BEST SUPER BOWL
FINISHES

by Paul Bowker

www.12StoryLibrary.com

12-Story Library is an imprint of Bookstaves.

Photographs ©: Charlie Riedel/Associated Press, cover, 1, 4; Allen Kee/ESPN, 5; Kathy Willens/Associated Press, 6; dean bertoncelj/Shutterstock.com, 7; Gene Puskar/Associated Press, 8; Ezra Shaw/Getty Images, 9; Paul Spinelli/Associated Press, 10; Ron Foster Sharif/Shutterstock.com, 11; Matt Slocum/Associated Press, 12; Paul Spinelli/Associated Press, 14; Michael Tipton/CC2.0, 15; Bernard Gagnon/CC3.0, 16; Paul Spinelli/Associated Press, 17; JOHN GAPS III/Associated Press, 18; Action Sports Photography/Shutterstock.com, 19; Phil Sandlin/Associated Press, 20; Al Messerschmidt/Associated Press, 22; Peter Read Miller/Associated Press, 23; Unknown/PD, 24; Focus on Sport/Getty Images, 25; Uncredited Associated Press, 26; ncbronte/CC2.0, 28; Au Kirk/CC2.0, 29

ISBN
978-1-63235-543-0 (hardcover)
978-1-63235-661-1 (ebook)

Library of Congress Control Number: 2018946726

Printed in the United States of America
Mankato, MN
June 2018

Access free, up-to-date content on this topic plus a full digital version of this book. Scan the QR code on page 31 or use your school's login at 12StoryLibrary.com.

Table of Contents

Super Bowl LI: New England Patriots vs. Atlanta Falcons

The Super Bowl had never seen an overtime. Quarterback Tom Brady and the New England Patriots changed that in Super Bowl LI in 2017. The Patriots scored 31 consecutive points to defeat the Atlanta Falcons 34-28 in overtime. They trailed the Falcons 28-3 in the third quarter for one of the greatest comeback victories in Super Bowl history.

Brady passed for 466 yards and two touchdowns. He was the first quarterback to throw for that many yards in a Super Bowl. The Patriots tied the game with 57 seconds left when Brady threw a two-

point conversion pass to Danny Amendola. Patriots running back James White won the game with a 2-yard touchdown run in overtime. This was the fifth Super Bowl championship for Tom Brady.

Brady led the Patriots to a touchdown or field goal in five straight possessions. The last three were touchdowns. Meanwhile the Patriots held the Falcons to zero points in the last quarter and in overtime.

546
Yards run by the New England Patriots in Super Bowl LI.

- The Patriots scored 31 consecutive points to beat the Atlanta Falcons in overtime.
- Patriots quarterback Tom Brady won his fifth Super Bowl.
- Super Bowl LI was the first overtime game in Super Bowl history.

A WINNING CONNECTION

Tom Brady of the New England Patriots is the first NFL quarterback to win five Super Bowl championships. He was with Patriots head coach Bill Belichick for every one of them. Belichick believes that Brady is the best quarterback of all time. The two of them meet twice a week on a game week to discuss strategy.

Super Bowl XLIX: New England Patriots vs. Seattle Seahawks

The Seattle Seahawks had one yard to go to win Super Bowl XLIX. They trailed the New England Patriots by four points with less than one minute remaining. The ball was on the Patriots 1-yard line and the Seahawks were expected to run. A touchdown was nearly certain. Instead, the Seahawks attempted a pass which turned out to be a bad decision.

THINK ABOUT IT

Do you think the Seattle Seahawks coach Pete Carroll made the right call in attempting a pass? If not, which play would you have attempted? Would you have called a timeout? Why or why not?

Seahawks quarterback Russell Wilson tried to throw the ball to Ricardo Lockette. Malcolm Butler was a rookie cornerback for the Patriots. He jumped in front to intercept the pass.

The interception happened in the final minute of play. It was the biggest play of the season for him. Butler was undrafted out of college and signed to a rookie contract. However, his interception clinched a victory for the Patriots over the Seahawks, 28-24. It was one of the biggest defensive plays in 2015. And in Super Bowl history.

4

Touchdown passes made by quarterback Tom Brady in Super Bowl XLIX.

- A Seattle Seahawks attempted pass in the final minute was a bad decision.
- Quarterback Russell Wilson's throw was intercepted by Patriot's cornerback Malcolm Butler.
- Butler's interception clinched the win for the Patriots.
- Seahawks running back Marshawn Lynch rushed for a game-high 102 yards.

7

Super Bowl XLVII: Baltimore Ravens vs. San Francisco 49ers

The 2013 Super Bowl goes down in history for several reasons. There was a power failure at the New Orleans Superdome. It happened just minutes into the third quarter. This game was also known for the infamous wardrobe malfunction in the halftime show by Janet Jackson and Justin Timberlake. However, a strong defensive stand in the final minutes delivered a 34-31 win for the Baltimore Ravens.

The 49ers had the ball at the Baltimore 5-yard line with the game on the line. A sixth Super Bowl win in franchise history was close enough to taste for the 49ers. But they were unable to score. The 49ers attempted to score three consecutive times on passes. Each

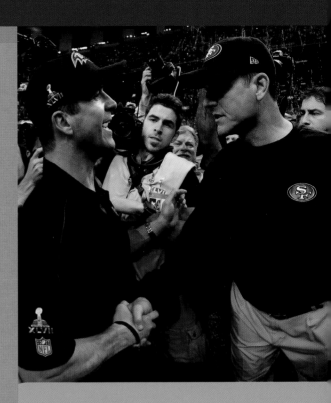

13

Number of Pro Bowl selections earned by Baltimore Ravens linebacker Ray Lewis.

- Super Bowl XLVII had a power failure and an infamous halftime show.
- The Baltimore Ravens stopped the San Francisco 49ers at the 5-yard line to win.
- The 49ers attempted three passes to win the game, but each fell incomplete.

pass fell incomplete. On the last play, San Francisco quarterback Colin Kaepernick tried to connect with receiver Michael Crabtree. But Crabtree was held by Ravens defender Jimmy Smith. 49ers coach Jim Harbaugh protested, but the play stood. The Ravens won the Super Bowl.

This was also Ravens linebacker Ray Lewis's last game before retirement. He started the night with a motivational speech to his teammates. It worked.

BROTHER VS. BROTHER

Super Bowl XLVII produced the first brother act in Super Bowl history. John Harbaugh was head coach of the Baltimore Ravens. Jim Harbaugh was head coach of the San Francisco 49ers. The brothers shared a firm handshake after the game. John said later that walking across the field to meet his brother was one of the hardest things he's ever done.

Super Bowl XLVI: New York Giants vs. New England Patriots

The drama of Super Bowl XLVI reached an incredible high. There were only 57 seconds left in the 2012 game between the New York Giants and New England Patriots.

Ahmad Bradshaw scored on a six-yard run to give the Giants a 21-17

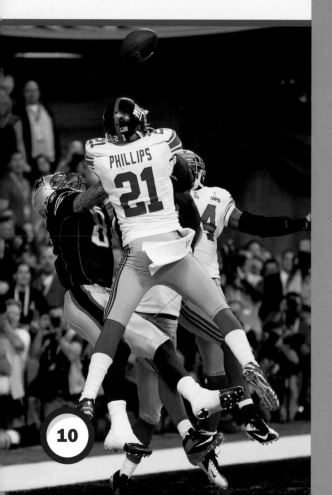

37:05

Minutes of possession by the New York Giants in Super Bowl XLVI.

- The Giants took the lead going into the final seconds of the game.
- New England Patriot quarterback Tom Brady set a Super Bowl record with 16 consecutive passes in the game.
- A Hail Mary pass lofted into the end zone by Patriots quarterback Tom Brady on the final play was knocked away.
- Super Bowl XLVI was the Giant's second Super Bowl win over the Patriots in four years.

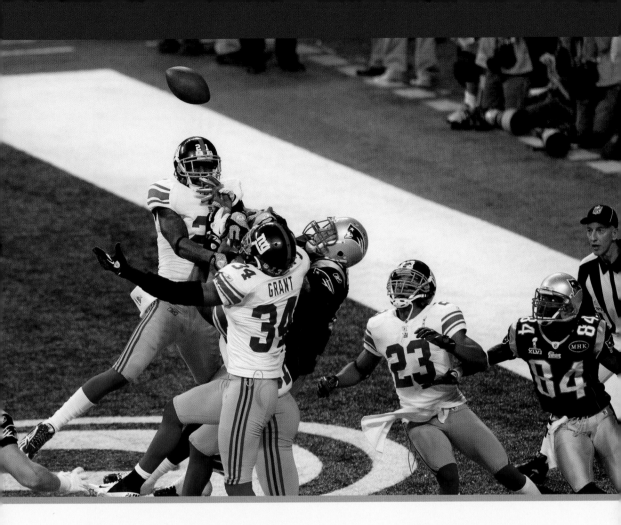

lead. Game over? Not when Tom Brady is quarterback.

The Super Bowl rivals had already delivered high excitement in 2008. The Giants handed the Patriots their first loss in a stunning Super Bowl upset. And now four years later, the Giants were attempting to duplicate their victory.

Brady had set a Super Bowl record in the game by completing 16 consecutive passes. And with the game on the line Brady had the ball in his hand. The Patriots were 49 yards away from the Giants end zone. Brady heaved a long Hail Mary pass into the end zone. The ball was headed to Patriots tight end Aaron Hernandez. Giants safety Kenny Phillips knocked the ball away.

The Giants celebrated. They had beaten the Patriots for the second time in four years.

Super Bowl XLIII: Pittsburgh Steelers vs. Arizona Cardinals

Pittsburgh Steelers wide receiver Santonio Holmes made one of the best catches in Super Bowl history in 2009. It was also one of the most controversial. Did Holmes have both of his feet down when he made a touchdown catch? There were only 35 seconds left in Super Bowl XLIII. It is a play that Arizona Cardinals fans would argue for years.

Arizona receiver Larry Fitzgerald had given the Cardinals a 23-20 lead on a 64-yard touchdown catch. But the touchdown made by Holmes gave the Steelers a 27-23 Super Bowl win over the Cardinals. The touchdown completed a 78-yard scoring drive for Pittsburgh. On the winning play, Steelers quarterback Ben Roethlisberger passed the ball over three defenders. The ball went to the corner of the end zone. Holmes went up on his tip-toes and reached out to catch the ball.

6
Record number of Super Bowl wins by the Pittsburg Steelers.

- A tip-toe touchdown catch by Santonio Holmes with 35 seconds left gave the Steelers the win.
- Holmes caught nine passes for 131 yards and was named Super Bowl MVP.
- Steelers head coach Mike Tomlin became the youngest coach to win a Super Bowl at the age of 36.
- The game was the third and last Super Bowl for Arizona Cardinals quarterback Kurt Warner.

In pro football, a catch is only legal if the receiver has both feet in bounds. It was ruled that Holmes had kept both toes in bounds. A perfect catch. And one of the most memorable catches in Super Bowl history.

6

Super Bowl XLII: New York Giants vs. New England Patriots

The New England Patriots were one game away from the perfect season. They had won their first 18 games. No NFL team had put together an unbeaten season since the 1972 Miami Dolphins. And then the Patriots ran into the New York Giants in the 2008 Super Bowl XLII.

The Giants produced one of the most stunning upsets in Super Bowl history. They did it with a touchdown in the final minute. And a helmet catch that would be talked about for years.

The big play was a catch by David Tyree on third down. Tyree somehow held the ball against his helmet as he went down. The play covered 32 yards. It gave the Giants a first down at the Patriots 24-yard line with 59 seconds left in the game.

Next, Plaxico Burress caught a 13-yard touchdown pass from Eli Manning with 35 seconds left in the game. It was a 17-14 victory by the Giants. Manning was the master in the game-winning drive that covered 83 yards. He was named the game MVP.

THE FINAL CATCH

New York Giants receiver David Tyree achieved fame with his helmet catch in the fourth quarter of Super Bowl XLII. It was his last catch for the Giants or any other NFL team. Tyree ended his NFL career with the Baltimore Ravens. He never made a catch in 10 games.

5

Number of times Patriots' quarterback Tom Brady was sacked in Super Bowl XLII.

- The New England Patriots won 18 consecutive games in the 2007 NFL season.
- Patriots' David Tyree made a helmet catch that gave the Giants a first down with 59 seconds left in the game.
- Plaxico Burress caught the game-winning touchdown pass with 35 seconds remaining.
- New York Giants quarterback Eli Manning passed for 255 yards. He was named Super Bowl MVP.

15

Super Bowl XXXVI: New England Patriots vs. St. Louis Rams

365

Total passing yards in a losing effort by St. Louis Rams quarterback Kurt Warner.

Finally, a Super Bowl was won on the last play. In 2002 the New England Patriots won over the St. Louis Rams 20-17. It began an impressive run of championships. The Patriots won three Super Bowl titles in four years. Until then they hadn't won any.

The Patriots were 14-point underdogs as they faced the St. Louis Rams quarterback Kurt Warner. Warner was the league MVP of 2001. The Rams tied the score at 17 with less than two minutes left

- The New England Patriots were tied with the Rams with less than two minutes left in the game.
- Brady moved the Patriots 53 yards to set Adam Vinatieri up for the winning kick.
- Vinatieri kicked a 48-yard field goal on the last play of the game to win the game.
- Patriots quarterback Tom Brady began his run of Super Bowl titles.

in the game. On the last play of the game, Adam Vinatieri of the Patriots kicked a 48-yard field goal to win the game. It was the first time in Super Bowl history that the game was won on the final play.

Patriots quarterback Tom Brady was named MVP in his first Super Bowl. The game began a run of Super Bowl titles for Brady and Patriots coach Bill Belichick. They won the championship five times from 2002 to 2017.

Super Bowl XXXIV: St. Louis Rams vs. Tennessee Titans

It is said that football is a game of inches. The Tennessee Titans discovered just how painful those inches can be at Super Bowl XXXIV.

The Titans were ready to win their first Super Bowl title in franchise history. They had the ball on the St. Louis 10-yard line with five seconds left. The Titans used their last timeout to set up their shot at a touchdown. Titans receiver Kevin Dyson ran a slant route across the field. Quarterback Steve McNair delivered the pass. Dyson caught the ball and headed for the end zone. But Mike Jones of the Rams brought him down.

Dyson tried to stretch the ball across the goal line. It was a yard short. It was one of the most dramatic ending plays in Super Bowl history. And for Tennessee fans it was a heartbreaking play. They were so close to winning a Super Bowl. Instead, the St. Louis Rams won 23-16.

THINK ABOUT IT

The play to Titans receiver Kevin Dyson missed winning a Super Bowl by inches. Let's make you the coach. Would you call for a different play to win the game? If so, what would it be?

41

Total receiving yards by Kevin Dyson of the Tennessee Titans in Super Bowl XXXIV.

- The Titans were ready to win their first Super Bowl with five seconds left in the game.
- Mike Jones of the St. Louis Rams stopped Kevin Dyson one yard short of the end zone on the final play of the game.
- Rams quarterback Kurt Warner passed for 414 yards and two touchdowns. He was named MVP.
- Rams receiver Isaac Bruce made six catches for 162 yards.

Super Bowl XXV: New York Giants vs. Buffalo Bills

The Buffalo Bills trailed the New York Giants by just one point. They were trying to win their first Super Bowl in the 1991 championship game played in Tampa, Florida. Bills kicker Scott Norwood lined up for a 47-yard field goal. Just four seconds were

A SUPER BOWL RECORD THAT NO TEAM WANTS

When the Buffalo Bills played the New York Giants in Super Bowl XXV, it was the first Super Bowl game in Buffalo history. They lost that game by a point. And then the Bills went on to win the next three American Football Conference championships. They lost the Super Bowl each year. No other team has lost as many Super Bowls.

5

Number of field goals made by Scott Norwood in the postseason for the 1990 Buffalo Bills.

- The Buffalo Bills were trying to win their first Super Bowl in the 1991 game.
- Bills kicker Scott Norwood tried to win the game with a 47-yard field goal, but missed.
- Giants kicker Matt Bahr booted a 21-yard field goal for the winning points in the fourth quarter.
- Giants running back Ottis Anderson ran for 102 yards and one touchdown. He was named game MVP.

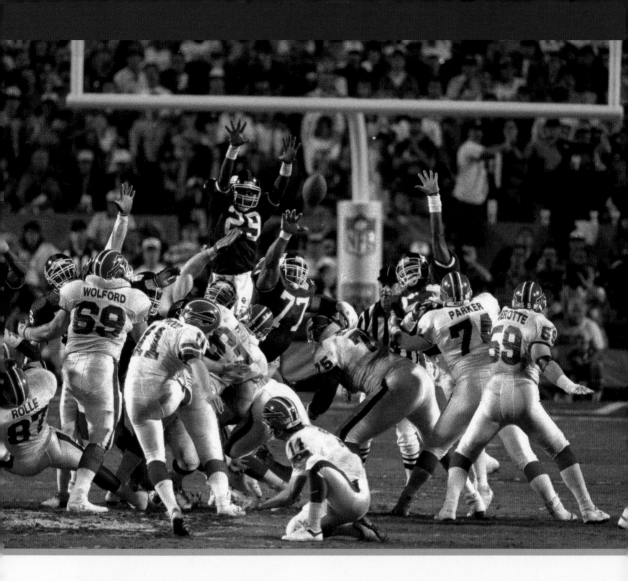

left. This would be the final play of Super Bowl XXV. The Bills and their fans were prepared to celebrate one of the best finishes in Super Bowl history. But the kick went wide right. The Giants won, 20-19.

Bills coach Marv Levy consoled his kicker. He explained that less than 50 percent of kicks that long are made. Bills teammates also comforted Norwood. What was lost in the missed kick by Norwood was that Matt Bahr won the game for the Giants. He had kicked a 21-yard field goal in the fourth quarter.

Norwood played one more year for the Bills before retiring. He hit two kicks of more than 50 yards in the following regular season.

Super Bowl XXIII: San Francisco 49ers vs. Cincinnati Bengals

The day belonged to San Francisco 49ers receiver Jerry Rice. The 1989 Super Bowl MVP caught 11 passes for 215 yards. He set a new Super Bowl record. But 49ers quarterback Joe Montana went in another direction to win Super Bowl XXIII. He completed a 10-yard touchdown pass to John Taylor. There were seconds left in the game. The dramatic play gave San Francisco a 20-16 victory.

Jim Breech kicked a 40-yard field goal. It gave the Cincinnati Bengals a 16-13 lead with 3:20 left. Montana completed eight out of nine passes for 97 yards in the winning touchdown drive.

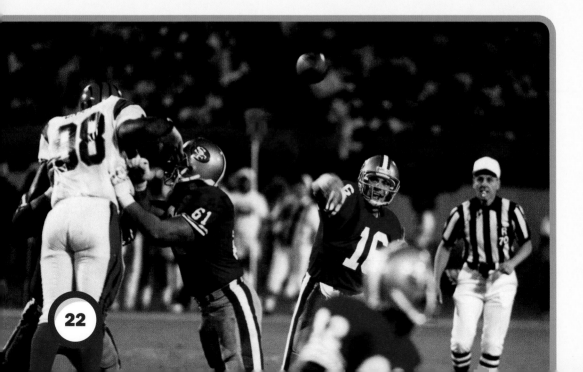

Rice had a career day. The Hall of Famer played in 29 playoff or Super Bowl games during his career. And this was his biggest day. Montana passed for 357 yards and two touchdowns. One of the scoring passes went to Rice and the other to Taylor. And when Taylor caught the game-winning pass, it was his only catch of the game.

34

Seconds left in the game when John Taylor caught a pass from Joe Montana to win Super Bowl XXIII.

- Super Bowl MVP Jerry Rice caught 11 passes for 215 yards, a new Super Bowl record.
- Stanford Jennings scored the Bengals' only touchdown on a 93-yard kickoff return.
- 49ers quarterback Joe Montana made a 97-yard touchdown drive.
- John Taylor caught the game-winning catch, his only catch of the game.

UNBEATEN IN SUPER BOWLS

San Francisco 49ers quarterback Joe Montana won every Super Bowl that he played in. He led his team to four championships and was selected game MVP in two of them. The win over the Cincinnati Bengals in Super Bowl XXIII was his third in eight years. The 357 yards he passed for in that game was his career high in a Super Bowl. Montana was inducted into the Pro Football Hall of Fame in 2000.

Super Bowl X: Pittsburgh Steelers vs. Dallas Cowboys

In 1976, the Dallas Cowboys were on a mission in Super Bowl X. They scored a touchdown in the game's final minutes to close the gap against the Pittsburgh Steelers. The Cowboys had trailed 21-10 in the final quarter. Now it was 21-17.

Dallas got the ball back with 1:22 left in the game. Quarterback Roger

Staubach led the Cowboys down the field again. But time was running out. On the final play of the game, Staubach threw the ball into the end zone. A catch by a Cowboys receiver would win the game for Dallas. He was trying to connect with Drew Pearson. Instead Glen Edwards of Pittsburgh intercepted the pass. The ball was deflected by Mike Wagner to Edwards. As the final sounded, Edwards ran out of the end zone with the ball.

It was the second Super Bowl win in a row for the Steelers. They joined the Green Bay Packers and Miami Dolphins as two-time Super Bowl champs in the first 10 years of the game.

161

Total receiving yards for Pittsburgh Steelers Lynn Swann in Super Bowl X.

- The Dallas Cowboys trailed the Pittsburg Steelers in the final quarter.
- An interception on the final play by Glen Edwards clinched a 21-17 win for the Steelers.
- The Steelers held on for the win with less than four minutes left in the game.
- It was the second consecutive Super Bowl win for the Steelers.

Super Bowl V: Baltimore Colts vs. Dallas Cowboys

Dramatic finishes did not describe the first four Super Bowls. None of the games were closer than nine points. Then came the Super Bowl V game-winning kick by Baltimore Colts Jim O'Brien in 1971. O'Brien kicked a 32-yard field goal with five seconds remaining to give the Baltimore Colts a 16-13 victory over the Dallas Cowboys.

It was a dramatic finish. But not a clean game. There were 11 turnovers in the game. Hall of Fame and NFL legend Johnny Unitas of

the Colts was intercepted twice. Cowboys quarterback Craig Morton was intercepted three times. O'Brien missed a field goal and an extra point in the first half. But then he made the winning kick to give the Colts their first Super Bowl championship.

It was the only Super Bowl that O'Brien played in. O'Brien was also a wide receiver for the Colts.

While O'Brien delivered the winning kick, the MVP award went to Dallas linebacker Chuck Howley. He had two interceptions. It is the only time that the MVP award went to a member of the losing team.

THINK ABOUT IT

Should the Super Bowl MVP have gone to the Colts Jim O'Brien for the winning kick? Or to Cowboys linebacker Chuck Howley? Very few defensive players win the MVP award. Why?

5

Number of turnovers in the fourth quarter of Super Bowl V.

- Jim O'Brien kicked a 32-yard field goal with five seconds remaining to win the game for the Baltimore Colts.
- There were 11 turnovers in the game.
- Dallas Cowboys linebacker Chuck Howley was named game MVP.
- It was the only time the MVP award went to a player on the losing team.

Making the Play

Minutes before his game-winning catch in Super Bowl XLIII, Santonio Holmes of the Pittsburgh Steelers made something clear to quarterback Ben Roethlisberger. He wanted to win the game. "I said to [Roethlisberger] that I wanted to be the guy to make the play for this team." That is precisely what happened. Holmes made the touchdown catch with 35 seconds left that won the game.

A "No Tech" Family

The helmet catch by David Tyree of the New York Giants in the winning drive of Super Bowl XLII is a video that has been viewed over and over again. Tyree somehow held on to the ball when it was lodged against his helmet. The Giants went on to score a touchdown to knock off the New England Patriots. Tyree had no idea the catch was replayed so often on TV. He says his family of nine does not have a TV. His seven children do not have smart phones, tablets or video games either. Instead, they read books.

Tackles Missing

Chuck Howley of the Dallas Cowboys became the first non-quarterback and the first member of a losing team to win the Super Bowl MVP award in 1971. He had two interceptions in Super Bowl V. How many tackles? That is unknown. The number of tackles weren't tracked in the NFL until 1979.

The Belichick Boat

New England Patriots coach Bill Belichick names his boat after his Super Bowl championships. He changed the name on the back of his boat to "VII Rings" after the Patriots defeated the Atlanta Falcons in Super Bowl LI. It was his fifth Super Bowl title with the Patriots. He also won two as an assistant coach with the New York Giants.

Taking a Break

When the power went out in Super Bowl XLVII some of the players simply laid on the turf. It took more than a half hour for the lights to come back on in the Mercedes-Benz Superdome in New Orleans. An international broadcast of the game was interrupted. Energy officials said the outage occurred because sensing equipment detected an abnormality.

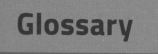

Glossary

end zone

The portion of the field where touchdowns are scored. It is 10 yards long and located at both ends of the field.

field goal

When a player kicks the ball between the two uprights in the goal post. A field goal is worth three points.

interception

When the football is grabbed by a player from the opposing team.

linebacker

A defensive player who is positioned behind the scrimmage line. They make tackles on both running and short passing plays.

MVP

Abbreviation for most valuable player.

quarterback

A player who runs the offense. They take the ball on a snap from the center. The quarterback usually passes the ball or hands it off to a running back..

reception

The catch of a pass thrown, usually by the quarterback. Receivers and running backs make most of the pass receptions.

running back

A player who lines up in the backfield with the quarterback. Their job is to receive the ball from the quarterback and run with it. Or they may also catch a pass or block for another player who has the ball.

slant route

A pass route run by a receiver. The receiver crosses the field at a slant so the quarterback can throw the ball to them in front of defenders from the other team.

touchdown

When a player with the ball gets into the end zone. A touchdown is worth six points.

turnover

When the defending team gets the ball with an interception or from recovering a fumble.

Books

Howell, Brian, *12 Reasons to Love Football*, Mankato, MN: 12-Story Library, 2018.

Scheff, Matt, *Amazing NFL Stories: 12 Highlights from NFL History*, Mankato, MN: 12-Story Library, 2016.

Hetrick, Hans, *The Super Bowl: All about Pro Football's Biggest Event*, North Mankato, MN: Captstone Press, 2012.

Visit 12StoryLibrary.com

Scan the code or use your school's login at **12StoryLibrary.com** for recent updates about this topic and a full digital version of this book. Enjoy free access to:

- Digital ebook
- Breaking news updates
- Live content feeds
- Videos, interactive maps, and graphics
- Additional web resources

Note to educators: Visit 12StoryLibrary.com/register to sign up for free premium website access. Enjoy live content plus a full digital version of every 12-Story Library book you own for every student at your school.

Index

About the Author

Paul Bowker is an editor and author who lives on Cape Cod in South Yarmouth, Massachusetts. His 35-year newspaper career has included hundreds of NFL games. He is a national past president of Associated Press Sports Editors and has won multiple national writing awards.

READ MORE FROM 12-STORY LIBRARY

Every 12-Story Library Book is available in many fomats. For more information, visit 12StoryLibrary.com